I Am Listening
A Collection of Short Stories

Andrew Maina

Published by Biqil Publishers
Email; biqilpublishers@gmail.com
Tel; 0722 220 147

Designed by I. Oluoch Otieno

First published as a E-book in 2012 by Amazon
First printed as a paper back in 2019

ISBN 978 9966 133 77 9

Email; andrewmaina2010@yahoo.com
P.O. Box 3990, 01002
Thika, Kenya
Tel; 0721 518 616

Printed & bound by
Edgly Brandz Ltd.
P.O. Box 77484
Nairobi
Tel; 0722 810 994
Email; info@edglybrandz.co.ke

Dedication

To Euticus Kamau

Acknowledgement

I give thanks to the Almighty God for granting mercies of putting together this work for the honour and glory of His holy name.

I would also like to acknowledge the support I received from my family, especially Purity, my wife who patiently went through the first draft with all the mistakes and errors it contained.

I cannot forget Canon Prof. Wangari Mwai who has sacrificed her time in reading and editing this work more than three times. Her suggestions and support have also made my work easy. To Bishop Mulandi, who has taken time from his busy diary and gone through this work and even availed his comments.

Another special mention goes to Gituma M'Ikiara, my publisher for his professional advice and encouragement, to I. Oluoch Otieno and Lucas Kimani for the designing of this book, to Tabitha for her typing services and to the printer, Susan Mukami of Edgly Brandz.

Last but not least is to the many others not mentioned whose support enabled this work see the light of the day. May the Lord bless you all.

Andrew Maina
Author

Foreward

In the days when there were no television sets in our homes, many families spent their evenings listening and telling stories as they waited for the food to cook. These story telling sessions would at times go on until late after dinner. The stories were either real or fictional but always instructional. Above all, they were enjoyable and entertaining!

The TV has stolen all that! However, I believe that a family that wishes to stay instructed, and at the same time enjoy their evenings, this piece of writing by Maina is very ideal. I found it very enjoyable not only for individual reading, but also for the whole family. The children would greatly enjoy these stories before going to bed.

These are real life experiences of people Maina has known in the path of his life, while others are from his life experiences with his family. They are captivating stories. Once you start reading them, it becomes hard to put the book aside till you read the very last story.

I highly recommend it, not only for the schools, but also for the home library.

Bishop Dr. Henry Z. Mulandi
Christian Church International

Introduction

'*I Am Listening, a Collection of Short Stories*' is a collection of twenty eight (28) exciting, motivating short stories. They are so true to life that one cannot help to identify with them. The title is derived from the second story which is hilarious in its narration of how the fear of the mythical Cain of the Bible would make the young children call upon their parents, in this case the mother to escort them to attend to the call of nature at night.

Like all the other stories in this collection, this one is drawn from real life biographical experiences of the author and his village mates and peers. The faith in the protection from the mother is found in the fact that although the mother may fall asleep as one answer to the call of nature, the child will feel protected since the mother is "listening".

The major strength in these stories is the reference to the personal experiences of the author. The use of the pronouns 'I" and 'My" are evidences of this, and it captures the reader's attention. The experiences are not utopian but very close to the life of all who read them. Having grown up in the rural areas, I really found it easy to identify with the issues addressed in these stories.

All the stories have a religious inclination with a moral for the young readers. The stories are also told in simple and interactive English that is a joy to read.

Canon Prof. Wangari Mwai
Anglican Church of Kenya,
Deputy Vice Chancellor Students' Affairs,
United States International University (USIU))

Contents

The Rich Orphan   8
I Am Listening   12
Stolen Husband   17
Scars   20
The Slippery Roof   22
The Road Accident   25
The Dog is not Fed   28
The Guard   30
Chapattis for Christmas   33
Injection   37
Toothless Monkey   40
Sabina   43
Forgiveness   46
The Market Day   49
Black Tea Party   51
The Driving Lesson   55
The Rado Watch   57
I Will Marry Rhoda   60
Inheritance   63
The Man Who Arose   67
Angela   70
The Shepherds   71
Who Made the Decision?   74
The Push   80
Copy Cats   83
A Tribute to George   86
Baby Gacheri   89
Pupu   92

The Rich Orphan

I had known the catholic nun who took care of the orphaned children for about six months. As we sat and talked, she would issue an order or even a reprimand to any of the children who played a short distance from us on the dusty courtyard.

This was at St. Teresa Montessori Nursery School, which is located opposite the Robert Ouko Estate, in Kisumu City. For the last three years or so, this school had been the home of several orphaned children from the surrounding areas, especially the sprawling slums.

I cannot say that the home was run down for it was not supposed to be a children's home in the first place. It was basically a school. To be accurate, I would rather say that most, if not all the physical facilities for such a home were lacking!

The kitchen was a make shift iron-sheets shed, where the traditional three stones served as the stove, while the dusty courtyard in front of this kitchen is where they sat as they took their meals. Do not ask me what they did when it rained!

I was told that the bigger children lined the eaves of the dormitory while the little ones squeezed into their small sitting room. The dormitory, which could have been a refuge in such a time, was congested and had the smell of urine all the time. This was despite the great efforts by the nun and her staff in keeping the place clean.

Apart from the physical facilities, gathering food for these children was hard. The nun confessed that there were many occasions when they had nothing in the store for the next meal. "But the children have never slept hungry. Miraculously, a donation comes in on such a day. This was God's doing". The nun confessed.

The youngest child in this home was a baby of six months while the oldest was a boy of ten years or so. They were lovely children and their smiling faces a testimony of the love that boiled deep in their tender hearts. The Sister as they popularly called the nun knew all the hundred-plus children by name and could tell of their background without making a reference to her records.

"The children's department intends to bring another child to this home despite the problems we are facing," she told me.

She was narrating one of the happenings of the day that was coming to an end. Despite the current desperate situation in the home, a needy child was being moved from another home. I could not comprehend the logic behind such a move.

The officers from the department argued that the girl who was HIV positive, would receive a better care in this dilapidated home. I did not get an opportunity of visiting the home she was moving from, but could imagine its status. It is my prayer that more people will be touched and share the burden of looking after these children.

I was there when the child was delivered in a government vehicle at around six in the evening. She was a girl of eight years and carried her belongings in the common black paper bags. I am not talking of the tough carrier bags in which we carry groceries from the super markets. No. This was thin and delicate and could barely deliver home a single pineapple!

The sister was to tell me later that in the paper bag was a dress and a pant. Apart from the clothes she wore, that was all she owned. It was not a lot and I had initially thought that whatever she carried was in addition to whatever else she owned!

She was taken to the dormitory and I assumed shown the bed in which she would be sleeping. I also assumed that she must have been shown a place in which to keep her belongings! After a short while, the girl emerged and came over to us. She respectfully greeted me and then handed to the Sister 'a whole five shilling' coin!

"I had been given this to buy sweets," the girl explained as she handed over the coin.

"Thank you. I will add some more coins and buy bread for everyone," the sister answered as she put the precious coin into her pocket.

The girl retreated to the dormitory to start her new life with new friends, while I continued sitting like a statue going through an emotional turmoil. I was so touched by this act that I was at the point of shedding tears. After a moment, I took control over my emotions for I did not want to look foolish in front of the innocent children.

The girl had no obligation of handing over the coin and she could have simply kept it among her clothes. What drove her into surrendering it? I asked myself. The fact that she was an orphan and HIV positive counted little in my emotions, for such cases were many in this home already. In fact one could not tell the ones who were HIV positive from the ones who were negative.

What moved me was the simplicity in which

the girl responded to the love shown by the nun who had just received her. From her simple 'five shillings' action, I clearly understood that all (not most of) problems and the suffering we see around us could to be solved if love is applied.

With love, people would give without looking at the amount they have given, the number of times they have given or the amount left after giving. Apart from these, people would no longer be blind to the needs around them. No wonder the Bible declares that loving our neighbour is the greatest commandment next to loving our God.

I Am Listening

I grew up in Kandara, which is a distance of fifty kilometers from the City of Nairobi. Life in the village was comfortable and exiting as we moved from one day to the next. Our demands in life were very basic. A long tailed khaki shirt was all we needed to cover our nakedness. For us, a pair of shorts (leave alone a trouser) was a luxury far beyond our reach, and bothered us not.

An under pant was an item that many of us wore as we joined the high school. Those were the days when, 'Bond 007' type was in fashion. We stuck our shirt beneath them, and at the same time made sure that the pants were pulled way above the waistline of the shorts we wore. If we didn't do this, how else was the world to know that we were wearing an under pant?

Apart from attire, food was another thing that did not bother us a lot. To us, 'food was food'. We were not concerned with what was put before us, or the method in which it was prepared. For instance, if it was the season of green maize, we could eat it cooked, in any form; Shelled or unshelled, mixed with beans or plain.

Our taste was simple and could clear away whatever was laid before us and still ask for more! We would then go to bed with our protruding tummies full, and wake up the following morning to a breakfast of whatever remained after dinner.

We had many activities to keep us busy but many of them depended on the prevailing weather conditions. During the rainy seasons, mud skiing would be one of the popular game while swimming and fishing would be preferred in the hot season.

It is not my intention to paint a picture of us in joy and happiness all the time. No. We wept and suffered at times. For those who misbehaved during the day, a proper beating was the ultimate reward, most likely early in the evening. Due to our busy activities, such a beating was usually forgotten by the following morning. We were generally a happy lot.

Our house was built on an incline that went all the way down to the river. All the other necessary structures were built around it with the pit latrine pushed furthest in the compound. It was a simple iron sheet shelter, built above the pit that made the latrine.

A hole in the center of the room gave an access through which one released the 'canons'. They fell with a heavy thud in the dark bottom-less pit. Some bluish flies reigned in this room. You could see them fighting for space on the rims of this hole. This is the spot where the misfired cannons 'kissed the mouth' of the hole. The stench that issued from this hole was uncomfortable but we were not particularly bothered.

The number of times that one visited this shelter depended on the kind and amount of food that one had eaten. Under normal circumstances, such visits were made during the day. However, the routine could be broken especially during the season when fresh beans were in plenty.

Beans, more so the fresh ones, have a way of disorganizing the stomach! In some acute cases, one was forced to spend his or her time near a toilet. This was necessary for one could soil him or herself before reaching the enclosure. The situation would get desperate during the night. The journey to the toilet required courage which none of us had in the dead of the night.

Our imaginative minds conjured all sorts of images of what could consume us in case we ventured out of the security of our mud house, especially when alone. The wild animals were one of our worries.

There were always rumours that a leopard had been spotted in one of the big trees in the village. As a matter of fact I was to see a 'real' leopard years later when the school took us to the National Museum.

This was a dry-dead-leopard mounted on a stand! It unblinkingly stared at us.

The other thing that we dreaded in the darkness was an apparition. The most chilling was that of 'Cain'. I had never met Cain, nor had I met anybody that had ever encountered him personally!

However the possibility of crossing paths with this Old Testament's 'night runner' whose head we heard touched the clouds was not very comforting. It dimmed any urgency of venturing into the darkness.

Unlike the current situation where criminal activities are reported all over, crime in our village was very low. Thus the fear of thieves and robbers could not inhibit our movements in the darkness. In fact thieves of those days were cowards. They scampered away even before the opening of the door.

After feasting on beans or any other stuff for supper that disorganizes the stomach, the urgency of visiting the latrines in the middle of the night would arise.

As our father was rarely home, one would call the strongest person in the house, our mother.

She was a remarkable lady who could go out at any time of the night. Holding a lantern in one hand, she would be belting out her favourite song of the day. She feared nothing and amazed us with her courage.

"Mami," one would weakly call out.

"Mami," this time louder one would call.

"What is it?"

"Take me to the latrine."

"You go on. I am listening," she would answer. This assurance that she is listening would not be assuring enough and one would call again.

"I told you that 'I am listening'. You go ahead, I am not asleep. Take the lamp."

One would take the lamp as instructed and if lucky, pull along a companion with whom one shared the bed. With shaking legs and eyes vainly penetrating the thick darkness, we would go out. Our ears would at the same time pick any sound in the darkness. We would survive the dangers that hang in the darkness and make it to the latrine.

Both the 'escort and the escorted' would then tightly lock themselves into the latrine. With the mission accomplished, we would with fear and trepidation inch by inch, open the door to the latrine, scanning the darkness beyond the light of our lamp. With no looming danger noticed, we would dash to the safety of the house.

The assurance that my mother was listening was enough to give us courage to overcome our fears. There was even a likelihood that she would be fast asleep by the time we got back to the house!

This brings to the fore the assurance that our God is with us, and will never forsake us. All what we need is to believe in this assurance.

Why then do we suffer anxiety over issues that are beyond our control? It is because we waver in our belief and allow doubt to steal into our minds.

If the simple believe that my mother was listening could give us courage in the dangerous path to the toilet, how much more would our God protect in times of calamity? This is the God who never slumbers!

Stolen Husband

I cannot remember the circumstances under which I accompanied my sister-in-law in a visit to one of her old friends in Thika. Locating her residence was proving difficult for it had been a while since her last visit.

After walking around the estate for a while, we stood by a gate to compound that my sister–in-law thought to be our destination.

"We would like to see Mama Ciku," my sister-in-law requested the young lady who answered our knock.

"Which mama Ciku would you like to see?" I could see the puzzled look on my sister in-law's face. "There are two mama Ciku's in this home," the young lady offered as an answer to the question that was yet to be asked.

Without giving more details on her comment, she opened the gate and led us to the house. We were presently ushered into the comfortable sitting room and our handler disappeared somewhere in the big house.

On her return, she was in the company of another lady a little older than herself who held a baby in her hands. Another girl of around six years followed them.

"This is mama Ciku and behind her is Ciku," she said in introducing the woman and the young girl. We had not exchanged any word since our entry into this home but the confused look on my sister-in law's face intensified following the introduction. We shook hands and after a few pleasantries my companion expressed her fears that we were in the wrong house.

"You are not the Mama Ciku we were looking for," she explained about her connection with our 'mama Ciku' and that her husband worked with the Municipal Council.

The 'mama Ciku' who now sat in one of the seats across assured us that we were not really lost. It was only a small confusion. There was actually another mama Ciku and she would send for her if we were a bit patient. Presently, somebody was sent to call 'our mama Ciku' from a neighbouring house where she had gone on some errand.

I had not met the lady before but as soon as she entered the room two important things happened. One of them is that, the face of my sister-in-law lit up. Secondly, I noted that the two mama Cikus looked alike though one of them looked older.

The first mama Ciku excused herself and on her return brought tea, which she served to all of us. Over the tea, the two women filled one another on the happenings in their respective lives since their last meeting. Eventually, the issue of the confusion we had gone through came up.

"My life has been one long hell for the last eight years or so," she commented with a sigh. We were quiet as we waited for her to continue.

"You must have met one of my younger sisters I housed as she attended a secretarial course here in town."

"I can vaguely remember."
"She is the mama Ciku who received you."

"Oh Yes. I noted that she resembles you."
"What happened?" My sister-in-law prompted.

"A relationship developed between her and

my husband resulting into a pregnancy. I had been suspicious over their movements but reprimanded myself for harbouring such evil thoughts over my sweet little sister! Little did I know that to her, I would lose my husband."

I knew that I was inhibiting a free chat between them and so excused myself and took a walk in the big compound. Later, my sister-in-law filled in the details. She had even been shown the scars that she had received while fighting for her husband.

"This home has been a 'Kosovo' and it is by God's grace that peace now prevails. I have accepted Virginia as my co-wife," the bitter lady had confessed.

"Many were the times I schemed on killing her but the worry of what would happen to my children once I got to Kamiti (prison) held me back."

"I have come to accept the situation in my marriage as it is. It has been tough but I no longer focus on my husband for my future. I look upon God and He has sustained me through this mess."

They now lived together in the same house. The official bedroom for the second mama Ciku is the same one she had occupied as a visitor. All the children shared the other bedroom and the servant quarters.

I was awed to see a person who had gone through such turbulent times and could still afford a smile. How she retained her sanity escaped my imagination.

What could you have done had you been in her situation? Left your home and reorganized your life afresh? Suffered a mental break down and end up in a mental hospital?

Or could you have committed a murder and booked an appointment with the hangman?

Scars

Very few men in African have the courage of parading parts of their bodies that need not to be displayed. This has nothing to do with our traditions because historically, we see a man whose body was scantly covered.

For instance, the Bushmen are still comfortable walking the jungle almost naked while nearer home, the Maasais are at home with a simple shuka (wrapper).

The parts of our body that we keep out of sight are not necessarily obscene or sinful to display.

However, we tend to think that they are not good looking for public display. A good example is the legs. While most of our sisters go a bit too far in displaying this part of their body, most of us are keen on keeping them covered.

What escapes my understanding is why a man should be drawn by such a display while tightly covering his own.

I am among those who keep their legs covered, but with a good reason; they are thin and covered with scars. Thus, they remain covered and up to now, have never found a good reason of exposing them beyond the precincts of my bedroom.

I can't imagine the fate of many men if partners were chosen on the basis of their legs! Many of us would remain bachelors.

However, I am one of the lucky ones for my wife recovered long ago from the shock that the first sight of this part of my anatomy brought. She has learned to live with 'them' but on condition that I keep them decently covered in public.

"Papa how did you get this scar?" One of my children has asked in the past.

"I was injured while running after a rabbit." I would then be bombarded with questions until I told the whole story of the hunting excursion. This is usually easy for each of the scars has a story to tell. They are memorials of my childhood experiences.

Each of these experiences was painful but also important is the circumstance under which I got the scar. While the pain was a part of the process, the scars represent the physical hurt that my body received.

More importantly, the scars declare loudly that I was once hurt, but am now healed. This is a shout of victory!

What about the hurt to our feelings? What scars do we carry in our hearts? Do the scars curtail our enjoyment to the gift of life? Are we ashamed of these scars and keep them covered? Alas! This is the day to put on our shorts and enjoy our freedom, for the scars declare that our bodies are healed.

The Slippery Roof

Like in many other parts of the world, football was one of the popular games in the days of our childhood. However, we played the game under very unfavourable conditions.

To start with, proper balls were hard to find and we had to use our ingenuity in putting together rags and other odd materials into something as round as a ball. Using a sisal twine, we would string together these materials into balls of any conceivable size.

As we made our balls as large as possible, we often forgot that a ball is supposed to be light and soft: A light and soft ball fly easily and is 'friendly' to the kicking foot! What we usually made was in many cases heavy and hard in texture.

The other unfavourable condition that we suffered was not of our making. It was the terrain in our home area which is hilly and getting a space that is fairly level difficult.

This made the courtyard in front of our house a prime area in which we played. It was not a very large space for one to kick a ball with all his or her might.

In fact, such a kick landed the ball on any of the earthen walls of the house or sent it all the way to the river. Making a trip to the river after every kick killed the excitement in the game, while the earthen walls peeled-off easily from the impact of our heavy balls.

As such, a careless football game left the walls scarred, which earned us the wrath of my mother.

Other than the tough heavy balls, the steep terrain and walls that peeled easily, the other impediment to our enjoyment of the game was the barbed wire fence that enclosed the paddocks.

During the game, the ball would from time to time roll into these paddocks. In our haste in retrieving it, one would either pass through or jump over the barbed wire fence (using the gate was cumbersome and a waste of our precious time!).

To this day the scars I received from the barbed wire attest to my active participation in this game.

All these obstacles were easy to handle when compared with the roof to our house. It was one of the few in our village that was made of iron sheets and had two tips similar to the letter 'M'.

Though pleasing to the eyes, this kind of a roof was hard to maintain as it always leaked from the ridges. This got worse when things (like our balls) blocked the gutters.

To prevent further damage, none of us was allowed on top of this roof and it was a crime to do so. A thorough beating was the wage for such an action.

Despite this penalty, the urge to retrieve a trapped ball and continue with our game was in many occasions too high. Thus, in the absence of our parents, we still went to the top of this roof.

One accident that revolved around our football and this roof vividly remains in my mind. It was in an afternoon when our game was interrupted by a slight drizzle.

Soon after it subsided, we resumed our game with a new gusto. Unfortunately, a careless kick landed our ball onto the forbidden roof.

Other than being illegal, we all knew that

climbing onto a wet roof was suicidal. However, the eldest among us volunteered, and up the roof he went. With little strain he recovered and threw the ball to us.

This was the easy part! Coming down was another thing altogether and by holding on to the edges of a loose iron sheet he laboriously made his way down.

Along the way, the roof became more slippery as his weight exerted pressure onto his legs. As the legs could not hold the weight on their own, some of the pressure was pushed to his hands, which held on the sharp edges of the iron sheet.

As he slid, the iron sheets cut into his hands which in turn started bleeding. His blood was now the grease between the hands and the iron sheets! With the two surfaces now greased, the speed at which he slid increased, which in turn increased the injury to his hands.

From time to time, the pain in his hands would force him to release his hold onto the iron sheets for a moment but his fears of falling off the roof would force him into snatching at the sharp edges of the iron sheet again.

He released and held onto the iron sheet from time to time as he progressively slid to the edge of the roof. He was bleeding and calling for rescue.

We helplessly watched as he finally fell off the roof with a thud. He broke his leg and his hands were severely injured.

With the help of our neighbours, we took him to the hospital and for the next three months or so, he lay immobile. All he could do was to watch as we played our favourite game.

Road Accident

Several years ago Western Peugeot Services popularly known as Wepesi was the premier means of transport to Kisumu from Nairobi. The fleet was well maintained and one was almost assured of arriving to his or her destination on time.

I lived in Kisumu and family commitments took me to Nairobi quite often. I was still a bachelor and stayed with a niece, a nephew and a son to one of my friends.

My taxi left Nairobi in the afternoon and one of my brothers had seen me off. The journey was expected to take around five hours and we were expected in Kisumu at around seven in the evening.

With me was my nephew who usually spent his vacation in Nairobi with his mother.

Tired and with a full tummy, I fell asleep even before we took the main highway. My siesta was disrupted a short distance from Naivasha by a heavy traffic pile up.

We gathered that a multiple accident involving a trailer and several passenger vehicles had occurred and many people had lost their lives. The trailer had lost control and rammed onto other on-coming motorists.

A few meters down the road, we saw the truck. It was still intact and appeared 'innocent' as to the cause of such a serious accident. Even if any damage had been caused, it could not be very extensive. I defended it.

My opinion was to change when I saw the

wreck it had left behind a few minutes later. There must have been a traffic jam with no elbow space to maneuver away from the crazy trailer.

With its protruding 'shoulder', the trailer had literally ploughed through some ten on-coming vehicles.

Among the casualties were the occupants of the Wepesi that had departed from Nairobi ahead of us. The driver who was now dead had apologized to me for missing a seat in his car! In fact, if I had been alone, I could have taken the only seat remaining.

"If only you had been faster over your lunch, we could have used the taxi that departed just ahead of us." I had blamed my nephew over the unnecessary delay in our departure and lamented as we waited for more passengers to take the remaining seats.

I could not believe my eyes when I saw the wreck of that taxi. It was extensively damaged and some of its passengers were now dead while the remaining ones lay in hospital beds.

Rescuers were busy trying to free those still alive and trapped in the mangled wrecks. Fifteen people had lost their lives on the spot while many others were in critical condition and admitted in a local hospital.

We proceeded on the journey but at a slower speed even though we had lost some time. At around seven o'clock our journey came to another stop in Kericho when the car developed some mechanical problems. The repairs took time and we arrived home towards mid-night, long after our scheduled arrival time.

Even before we entered the compound, the door was opened by my niece, and on her face was joy and relief. Not only were they awake, but several of our neighbours were in as well! In a short while, they explained to us the anxiety that had gripped the house, our neigbbours and the family in Nairobi since the news of the accident broke out.

Many calls had been made in search of any information on what could have happened to us.

They told us that the accident had featured prominently in the evening news, and since our car had left Nairobi at almost the same time as the ill-fated taxi, everyone feared that we could have been among the victims. This fear was enforced by our failure to arrive as expected.

Like those around me, I was disturbed by what could have happened had we boarded the ill-fated taxi. Could I be dead by now? Or could I have escaped?

My reasoning was blind to the fact that death is our companion in every moment of our life.

Surrounding us are situations or things that can cause our death in a twinkling of an eye. As I write this piece, how safe am I from the four walls and the roof that surround me?

With the knowledge that we could die at any moment, it will be easier to appreciate and thank the Lord our God for the gift of life.

On top of this, we will not allow opportunities of mending our relationship with those around us pass. We will also grab the opportunities that come our way of being kind and helpful to those around us.

Above all, we shall be good workers, doing what we ought to do, and never put off anything to tomorrow. What a better world would this realization bring!

The Dog is not Fed

Boys especially those in the rural areas can eat a lot of food. This I know because as a boy I grew up in a rural area. There were incidences when we ate a whole pot of *githeri* (boiled maize and beans) as a snack.

Not that we sat around the pot and ate the content at once, no. We would scoop a little with a calabash or even with our bare hands, and go back to our games or whatever we had been doing.

After four or five of such visits by four energetic boys with insatiable appetite, little or nothing would be left in the pot.

My mother would not complain over our uncontrolled eating, especially if we had done all our daily chores. After all, the food was meant for us. Apart from this, food was in plenty and an alternative for dinner would be found.

What my mother would not bother doing is cooking the second dinner. Those who had feasted on the pot of githeri would be forced to do the cooking.

The other thing we were good at was in loving our dogs. They guarded our homes during the night, and during the day assisted in our hunting.

Apart from hunting, they were useful in our herding. In our absence, the watchful dogs would not allow the animals invade the cultivated land.

These useful pets needed to feed regularly and in our home ate from the same pot with the rest of the family, though mainly in the evening.

Where the food was inappropriate, or too

valuable to be fed to the dogs (like chapattis), a little ugali (a mixture of flour and water) would be made for them.

There were many occasions when the food would be shared out and the portion for the dogs would be forgotten.

Each person would donate a little from his or her plate for the dogs. One of my brothers was not always comfortable with this.

He would receive his share of food and clear his plate before everybody else. With his plate clean, he would then feign surprise and announce that we had forgotten to feed the dog.

Using his empty plate he would then collect a little from all of us for the dog.

The Guard

Among the businesses I have tried my hands on is that of provision of security guard services. It proved to be the most challenging and I thank God for sustenance through all those years until I ceded my interest in the firm to another person.

I do not wish to enumerate the pitfalls of running such an outfit but would wish to point out one thing; the more labour intensive a business is, the harder it is to manage.

I consider myself to be on a prolonged holiday when I compare my life today with the days in the guarding industry.

In those days, I could not with accuracy predict what I would be doing in the next one hour. Anything could happen.

A summon by a client or an urgent visit to the local police station would be one of the calls I could be attending to.

Sitting in the office was a time of listening to the many problems, which afflicted the guards. Most of them related to money and were easily solved if I had some cash on me.

A popular opening line in such a request was 'my family went to bed hungry', or 'the landlord has locked my house'. Apart from their many 'money problems', the other prevalent problem was sickness.

The guard himself would be sick or a member of his family. An off duty of a day or two and some cash was all that was needed in the less serious cases.

At times, I felt frustrated by the many incidences

in which I was unable to solve some of these problems.

The major restraining factor was my poor financial strength. I was always broke and schemed daily on where to source for the extra cash needed to see me through the next day.

It was at times humiliating when I had to turn down a request for a few shilling loan; may be a loan to buy a calabash of porridge for a hungry guard.

Guards are human beings and created in the image of God just like you and me. We all know that God created the sun to light our surroundings as we 'subdued' the earth.

We also know that the night was created so as to provide an atmosphere in which we could rest. As such, we rest during the night.

Some night guards, just like other human beings, get involved in the day time activities while they should be curled-up in a bed fast asleep. Some do it routinely with the intention of covering the lost sleep later in the night, while on duty.

I could pardon a guard falling asleep on duty while in a sitting position. However, pardoning a guard who spread a mat (read discarded pieces of cartons) to sleep on was at times hard. Such a guard had planned on sleeping on duty even before he actually fell asleep.

In my routine and random patrols, I met these incidences quite often. The victims would usually apologize and swear that they will never repeat the mistake again.

However, I had to control my temper on several occasions where the victim denied that he had been sleeping and claimed to have been awake and alert. It would be my word against his. In this case, I would be the prosecutor and the judge. In order to safeguard my reputation of a 'fair judge' I would quietly withdraw the case and instead issue a caution.

Apart from the victims' claim of their innocence, others had even accused me of drunkenness while conducting these random spot checks. The allegations were untrue for I never took alcohol.

With these experiences, I got wiser and would (if possible) pick one of the belongings of a sleeping guard. I would use these items (may be a baton or even a shoe) as my exhibit while making an accusation the following morning or later.

In our day to day life, do we make mistakes and injure those around us. How do we react when these mistakes are pointed out to us? Do we accept them and seek forgiveness or do we protest while trying to prove our innocence?

Chapattis for Christmas

I was meeting a village mate in Thika on business sometimes ago. I had not seen him for a long time and we had a lot to talk about. This casual meeting over a cup of tea became a dinner one and we parted company past midnight.

We talked about many things among them the pre-independent Kenya. In the early 1950's most of the African continent was under the reign of foreigners.

Among them were the British, under whom the current Kenya fell. The Kikuyu and a few other neighbouring tribes revolted against their rule, mainly because the colonists had taken their land. A bitter guerilla war ensued and many people lost their lives on both sides.

To control the Africans during the night, the British imposed a curfew and everyone was supposed to be in his or her house at a particular time.

In managing the curfew more effectively, they moved the villagers from their ancestral land (maganjo) and forced them to live in one big village called gicici.

They would till their ancestral land during the day and return to the villages in the evening well before the time of the curfew. In as much as this step gave the British the control over the local people it also increased their hatred to the regime.

The villages were too large to secure by a fence or by posting guards all around. This made the colonialists move a step further. They forced the villagers dig trenches all around the villages leaving a space for two entrances. One led to the river while the second one joined the village with the rest of the world by a road.

The trenches were so wide and deep that any one falling-in needed to be rescued. To make it worse, sharp stick spikes were dug into their floors. Many people, including children lost their lives through such a fall. The other major casualties were livestock.

This period formed a major part of the history of the local people. As such, you could hear that so and so was born in the gicici, while another person in the 'maganjo.'

After the independence, the locals moved back to what was left of their ancestral land and rebuilt their old homesteads.

Though independence had been attained, the land, which had been taken from their hands and was the cause of the conflict, was never restored.

Thus there was always a need of adding to the little piece of land they owned (at least for those who could afford).

Those with no source of income, but still in need of a larger piece of land sold the little they had and moved to the rift valley region where good land was in plenty, and cheaper in price.

The village mate I was meeting was born in the 'gicici' and he went to class one in 1963, the year of our independence. When others were moving to their ancestral land, his family moved to the piece of land that his father had recently acquired. He emotionally disclosed to me that this land was bought with a loan from my father.

As such, he took seriously my enquiry on land available for sale near his home in Thika. It was his turn to return the kindness that his father had received! This really touched me.

He was thankful for the Lord had favoured him in many ways. He had a good job and his family did not go through the hardships he endured in his childhood. As he narrated of his up-bringing, he lamented over the abject poverty they experienced.

"Both your father and my father worked in Nairobi."

"Yes." I nodded in agreement for this was not news to me. I knew that they worked with East African Railways and Harbours.

He narrated an incidence that left bare the kind of poverty they experienced. He recalled clearly that it was around the month of October that his father sent a parcel home through my father. It was a packet of wheat flour: flour to be used in making chapattis in the coming Christmas festivities, a Christmas that was over two months away!

Chapattis were usually made to celebrate the birth of Christ and only the rich could afford this luxury at any other time of the year. However, I had never heard of anybody making such an early preparation for the festivities.

Several questions remained unanswered. For instance: how did his father acquire this precious product? Was it a present or did he buy it? Why did he have to send my father to deliver it while he could have waited for his next visit home?

Both men passed away several years ago (may they rest in eternal peace) and I can only guess the answers to these questions. However, the fact that my village mate could remember this kindness shown to his parents really moved me. It gave me an opportunity of re-examining my life. How long do I remember the kindness shown to me? If I do, how often do I show kindness to those around me.

Injection

Several years ago I suffered from a severe sickness that required a constant medical attention. For two weeks, I was receiving injections at regular intervals. I thank the Lord for I fully recovered and have for years enjoyed a good health.

That was a trying period because I was single and lived in a town far away from home. Apart from this sickness, I was going through hard financial times and depended on my friends for survival.

"These daily injections must run without any interruption at all. Otherwise you will have to repeat the whole process again," the doctor had warned even before he commenced the treatment.

Keeping these daily appointments was easy though my bottoms were already swollen after receiving a week's treatment. They were sore and many were the times when the spot that had suffered under the needle the previous day received a second visitation.

It was a painful experience and I came to dread this daily ordeal. Sitting down was now a torture to my aching body.

One of my friends even joked that my bottoms would be like a sieve by the end of the exercise! That did not worry me. All that I yearned for was getting well.

During the period of this treatment, I was compelled to travel to Mombasa on some important business. I was to be away for several days and had to make arrangements for my regular injections.

The doctor gave me the dose for the period, together with a prescription. These I would present to a medic to administer during the period of my travel.

To avoid the long bus ride to Mombasa, I traveled to Nairobi overnight hoping to take a connecting bus later in the afternoon.

That gave me a whole morning in which I was to see a relative who worked in Langata. Langata is way out of town and the trip to the city center was known for its traffic jams even in those days. However, I believed that I would have enough time to snake back for my bus.

At half past eleven I was still nosing my way to the round about joining Uhuru Highway and Haile Selassie Avenue. I was jittery and could not sit still. My destination was too near yet too far. I decided to alight and walk rather than endure the stress as the matatu inched its way.

Before I boarded my bus, I had to get the injection administered for I would be arriving in Mombasa late in the evening. I had already identified a building that hosted several doctors a short distance from the bus terminus to Mombasa.

I impatiently waited for the lift, which turned out to be the ancient type and in its chameleon-hurried movements, sighed as it made its way to my floor. I was stressed to a breaking point by the time I got the opportunity of presenting my problem to the nurse.

The nurse was sympathetic and attended to me immediately. To my surprise she declined the payment that I offered. Thanking her hastily, I rushed in the direction of the bus with just a few moments before its departure.

"I was in a hurry and was unable to thank you properly," I explained to the nurse a few days thereafter, as I handed over a paper bag containing some mangoes.

"Please remind me what I did to be honoured with such a present."

I was not embarrassed in reminding her of the circumstances under which we met, though surprised that she could not remember her heroic deeds. This incident brought to the fore the popular Swahili saying *'tenda wema nenda zako'*, which roughly translated means 'do good and go your way'.

What makes us enumerate our good deeds to those around us? Do we do enough? From today, I will aim at 'doing good and going away.'

Toothless Monkey

Matters related to death have very sobering effect on all human beings, and in losing a loved one, we realize how temporal life is. During such a time, even those who never go to church, get an opportunity of listening to the word of God.

I salute the preachers of the Good News for they have always made a good use of this opportunity. Thus, the mighty and lowly have been subjected to the at times ear blistering gospel and many have changed their lives for the better.

I attended the funeral of a friend a few months ago and the preacher talked of salvation in a way that was very captivating. He made it clear that salvation goes beyond a mere declaration.

"There lived a farmer in the neighbourhood of a forest." The preacher narrated.

"This farmer used to plant maize and other food crops which are a favourite to monkeys." The preacher went on to tell us that his efforts in protecting the crops against these animals were a failure.

Every season he would plant but a good part of the ripening crop would go to the monkeys.

"His land was fertile and the yields were always abundant especially when he protected the crops from the wild animals."

Any time he captured a monkey he would kill it and hang the carcasses on a stick which help little in protecting his crop. What it did was to attracted more monkeys to his farm as they came to mourn their dead relative.

As they mourned they would feast on the remaining crop in the farm. Other than attracting the mourners the killing of the animals was a messy affair that the farmer hated.

Before his retirement, the farmer used to work as a dentist and still kept some of his tolls of trade. He decided to be pulling out all the teeth of the monkeys that he captured. It was still an unpleasant task but at least no one would accuse him of killing the poor animals.

No matter how unpleasant the task was, he was not bothered by the cries of the trussed animal as he pulled the teeth. After all, he had endured such cries from the many patients he attended to in his career as a dentist.

"He would then release the toothless animals." The preacher continued.

The toothless monkey would be received with a relief by its relatives back in the forest. They would console him for the pain that he had endured and with time, the animal would heal and even resume its normal daily activity.

"Let us visit that farmer's maize plantation." In the coming seasons one of the monkeys would persuade the monkey whose teeth had been removed.

"I can't risk my life again. After all I can no longer eat maize!" The toothless monkey would answer.

"Yes, that is what I consider true salvation," the preacher declared, "the ability to separate ourselves from sin."

"What some of you need is a treatment like that of the monkey, the organ that make you sin should be removed."

"If you are a thief, the hands you use in stealing should be removed. If you persist in stealing, you may find your legs cut off as well. If you are a man and adulterer, then you know which of your organs need to be removed."

"If our lives are truly changed through salvation, it is time we saw all the things that displease God as sins. This ability of identifying sin will not only make as saved but will truly keep us safe."

"It is my prayer brethren that you will be thoroughly saved and that you will have the inability of sinning, just like the toothless monkey." The preacher closed his sermon.

Like the monkey, I ran my tongue over my teeth and for the first time realized how prone I am to sin.

Sabina

Sabina was my cousin and she could be in her late forties had she survived the delivery of her first and only child. David, the son she left behind, is now in his late twenties.

Our relationship went deeper than the proverbial 'blood is thicker than water'. This was after I became a teacher in the secondary school she attended. The double relationship of being a teacher as well as a cousin, gave her a special place in my heart. I was in that school for just a term and we did not have the opportunity of interacting a lot. A simple wave, a smile or a little chat when we met in the corridors was all we had.

Partly because of the short distance the school was from her home and the short period I was in the school, situations where I could have played heroic roles as a big cousin never arose. However, this did not in any way hinder the swelling of my feelings towards her. I still felt responsible over her welfare.

After barely a term in the school, I lost my job and with it, my contact with Sabina. I found my way to Nairobi and secured a job with a shoe company where the working hours were tight and the only free time I had was on Sundays.

I do not remember meeting Sabina again but I still received news on her progress. She had completed her secondary school education and moved to Nairobi where she was pursuing a course in one of the colleges. The next thing I heard was that she was pregnant and had actually moved in with a guy. Formal talks between their two families were in progress and everything about their relationship was official.

I should have mentioned that Sabina was a very attractive girl, comfortable in her deep black skin that had a white-powder-like sheen. She was a black beauty and stood out among all the girls in her class.

The next time I saw her was in Nairobi and at a distance. Both of us were crossing the street but headed to different directions. She was very heavy with a child and I can vividly remember that she was in a sky blue maternity dress.

The lunch hour traffic was heavy and I thought that I would draw her attention as soon as I reached the other side of street. This I did not do, and she was soon lost in the thick crowd. I shrugged off my good intention and consoled myself with a hope of giving her a visit soon.

Nothing serious could have happened had I missed my lunch neither could I have lost my job for reporting to work a few minutes late. Is it possible that I was unconsciously avoiding taking Sabina out for lunch? Maybe, maybe not. I could have hastened on my way for a thousand reasons but it all boils down to the fact that I failed in making an effort in contacting her!

That was the last I ever saw Sabina. A few days later, she passed away in pregnancy related complications. She had bled to death soon after giving birth to a bouncing baby boy. This news devastated me. I felt guilty that I had failed to make contact just a few days ago and mourned with bitterness towards myself.

The bitterness is gone but I realized that I should always try and seize the opportunities of doing good that come my way. Such opportunities are many in all the spheres of our lives. For a student, opportunities are many in his or her learning situation.

As we grow up and take up responsibilities, these opportunities abound. From a family setting, each of us can improve his or her relationship with those we love. Let us take these opportunities in loving our parents, our spouses, our children, or even our relatives better.

We dilly-dally and foolishly wait to do what could have been done today tomorrow. No wonder many of us live in regrets.

Forgiveness

A Minister in the church I attend delivers his sermon with parallels. This method drives home his lessons more easily. One Sunday, he told us of a visit to a busy dental clinic which was characterized by long queues day in, day out.

"Dental patients have the tendency of visiting the clinic early in the morning in contrast with other patients," the Minister narrated.

"This could be directly related to an overnight toothache whereby the patient anxiously waits for the daybreak. Apart from this, the confidence that the pain will go away once the irritating tooth is extracted may prompt such an early visit." continued the narration.

The dentist in this story worked hard and made sure that he attended to all the patients who flocked his clinic. One day, a man with a painful tooth queued like the other patients. He had a great fear of injections and in many occasions opted for oral medication. When his turn to receive the injection that numbs the tooth before its extraction came, he requested the doctor for an alternative medication.

There was no any other kind of medication and he reluctantly agreed to receive the injection. Still in fear, the patient could not sit still and allow the injection to be administered and any time the needle came near his mouth, he would turn his head and hold the hand of the nurse. This annoyed the dentist that he moved to the next patient.

Still in pain, the man left the clinic with a hope

of getting another dentist who would treat him in the way he wanted. After all, they were many dentists in his town. In his search he met with one of his friends who enquired on his welfare.

"Not good my friend," he answered in a mumbled voice, common with those suffering from a tooth ache. "My tooth is aching and the dentist has refused to treat me," he went on to tell of his tribulation in the hands of the dentists. Reluctantly, he disclosed that he had resisted the mandatory injection before the extraction could be done.

"Even if you visit another clinic, the same injection shall be administered. There is no way you can escape," his friend observed.

"You better go back and seek an opportunity to see this dentist again, after all you have already paid the consultation fee," his friend continued. The patient argued that the dentist could not agree to see him again but his friend urged him on.

Back to the queue his turn to see the dentist a second time came. As soon as the patient ahead of him stepped out of the examination room, the dentist in a clear voice shouted, 'next'. The 'next' patient entered and the dentist took his details and examined him a fresh. The dentist did not recognize him at all. To him this was the 'next' patient. This time the patient did not resist the injection like in the last incidence. A short while thereafter, the aching tooth was extracted and he went home relieved.

Are there times when we wrong those we are in a relationship with, and assume that the relationship we had is over? It is possible that our guilt has become a barrier with those we have wronged? It is even likely that those perceived enemies do not have anything in their heart against us. To get reconciled is easy. All that is required is for us to seek forgiveness. If this is too hard for us, let us do things which show our remorsefulness.

The Market Day

Mondays and Thursdays are the official market days for Kandara market. Apart from Sunday, the rest of the days of the week are shared out between the other two neighbouring markets. These are the Ndunyu Chege and Kangunduini markets.

Thus the major traders are able to offer their wares for sale from one market to the next throughout the week. This does not mean that no trading takes place in these markets during the rest of the week! Business continues as usual but the variety of goods on offer is limited.

During the designated market days, you will find a large number of people, both young and old, from near and far villages headed in this direction.

As a young boy, I thoroughly enjoyed the company of my mother on the many times we went to our trading center on the market days. Such a visit was an opportunity to feast on all the 'good things in life'.

Among them were mandazi (some kind of doughnut), sweets and ripe bananas. From these visits, I gained experience and with time could safely do the purchases on my own. That was heaven for me because the savings I made by vigorous bargaining, financed my personal purchases.

After my circumcision, my purposes in visiting the market changed. In fact, buying things in the market and carrying them home was not a job befitting a person of my stature! Anyway, I still went to the market but to meet girls who came shopping.

It is against this background that I visited this market many years later. I had nothing to buy nor was I looking for girls. In fact, I was in the company of my wife, who was to do all the shopping. We were staying in our rural home after the violence that erupted in many parts of the country after the elections of 2007.

The crowd was large as always, and the variety of goods to choose from broad. A nephew in our company briefed us on the various aspects of the market and even told us funny stories of some of the people we met on the way.

Among them was an elderly couple, walking home with two goats. There was nothing spectacular about them and I assumed that they had bought the animals.

We were informed that they were established traders in livestock. They bought and sold their animals together and at the end of the day, walked home together.

When their finances allowed, they would take a beer or two in their favorite pub before making their way home. In case they took too many beers and walking home became risky, the couple took a room in one of the lodgings for the night.

I may not like their drinking habits but I salute their commitment to each other. They have excelled where many have failed; they spend time together and no matter the inadequacies they may have, they still remain my heroes in marriage.

Black Tea Party

Jason's dream that his security guarding company would one day be profitable was slowly dying away. He was in debt and suffered from ever increasing cash flow problems.

At twenty-six and still single, he could have simply closed down and went back to his career as an accountant. But he could not let his ailing company go. Something urged him to hold on.

He was based in Kisumu and his office was a former kitchen, with all the fittings still intact. Though a small room of eight feet by five, Jason was still proud of the office he had occupied for three years.

As a trained accountant he had made his financial projections for the business, which made his heart run faster than normal. The figures were impressive and the future looked prosperous. However, his forecasts were blind to all the 'black spots' on his road to prosperity! For starters, he had not foreseen the fact that some of the clients would fail to pay on time, and that some of these debts would eventually graduate into bad debts.

The other 'black spot' that he was blind to was that clients would incur losses from time to time (not necessarily due to his guard's negligence). This would result in payments being withheld or lost depending on the circumstances under which the loss was incurred. All these and others pitfalls were eating into his 'prosperous future'.

These were some of the lessons he was learning

from experience. Jason had no problems with such a learning process but recognized that his ambition was drowning in this purported learning. Had he some financial back up, this learning could have been more bearable, and the deficit emerging easily covered. Jason had no one to run to.

Apart from the part-payment he had made as he took over the company, Jason had invested nothing else in this business. He assumed that he would be paid, and in turn pay the guards. The balance would be enough to pay the other business expenses and still remain with something for his allowances. This was a dangerous way of running a business, more so, a guarding company. It was by God's grace that the guards never clobbered him as they demanded their delayed salaries from time to time.

Though young and full of pride in his position as an almost successful businessman, Jason was to learn the art of humility. He had to be polite to those passing by the office demanding their pay. Many were the times that he felt drained of energy of facing a new day. On such a day, he could have easily kept away from the office, but this could have made the situation even worse.

With no money to pay and nowhere to run to, he sat in the office and pleaded with each guard as they passed through. At the same time, he shared the little that came his way. Walking home and sleeping without dinner was becoming a common thing to him. The situation was desperate and getting no better.

Members of his support staff were very understanding and they patiently waited for their pay without complaint. Apart from this, they contributed some money and purchased a kerosene stove with which they started making tea. This tea was nothing fancy but plain black tea *(turungi)*. When their finances allowed, they used to buy a loaf of bread and chase it down with the black tea. Many were the days when this tea served as his only meal for the whole day and night.

"The bosses enjoy themselves while we die of hunger," some guards were to complain over the tea. "It is our money they are using," others would fuel the anger over the tea.

Their complaints were genuine and he could not swear that it was not their money they were using. It was in fact one of the ways in which he mismanaged the finances of the company! Were they not enjoying their tea and bread while the salaries remained unpaid? This tea was turning into a major issue to the guards, a thing that perturbed him. How could he make them understand that he barely ate anything else for days, other than the tea and the dry bread?

As unreasonable as it sounded in his ears, the guards were right. They had the right to demand for their pay and he had failed miserably in meeting these needs. In fact, most of them were going hungry and could not even afford a cup of black tea!

Many guards moved to companies which paid salaries promptly which in-turn led to a biting shortage of guards. As a result many contracts were terminated. His business was shrinking and the projections were false! He only held onto the business for there was nothing else better that he could do. He had to persevere.

After several months, his financial situation stabilized and could meet his obligations as they came. With time, he was even getting some new business and regaining his lost glory.

Through these hardships Jason learned some important lessons in life. He came to understand that he had to be thankful for everything that was happening in his life, no matter how insignificant it may appear.

He also understood the thinking process of the guards and to some extent, the less fortunate. To him and the office staff, this tea was a means of survival.

This was different to a guard who faced the likelihood of spending the night in the cold and hungry. To such a guard, the cup of tea was all he needed.

Is it because we do not appreciate the seemingly insignificant good things happening in our life that we are continually complaining and lamenting?

Stop complaining and take a closer look at the people around you. You will find many who are worse off than you are. What seems ordinary to you may be very special to somebody else.

The Driving Lesson

The temperatures in Kisumu are at times hot for a person born and grown in the mild climate of Mt. Kenya. However the evenings are pleasant as the sun goes down.

It was on such an evening some twenty years ago, that I met Obiero for the first time. In our introductions I learnt that he was an engineer in an oil company which had just opened a branch in Kisumu.

I also learned that he had a few days ago bought a new car and he was still learning how to drive.

We had driven to his house with Ochieng, an old friend of mine who was conducting extra coaching in his driving lessons. The three of us entered into his car and he slowly drove to the leafy Milimani estate where the traffic is low and ideal for such lessons.

In the interactions between the instructor and the student, I learned that he had already acquired a driving license and all he needed was a few lessons.

This did not surprise me for many people acquired their driving licenses through the 'back door'. The lessons were over and we were headed to his home.

He was the one driving and the instructor asked for a can of beer that lay besides me.

"I would like to be taught on how to drive after drinking that," he was referring to the can of beer from which his instructor was drinking.

"That will be easy though expensive"
"Why?"

"You will be required to get both of us drunk"

"That does not worry me, when can we start?"

I was not present when the driving lessons under the influence of alcohol were conducted. However, I did enjoy their benefits many times when Obiero drove us home late in the night, dead drunk. He had become an expert driver, and bragged that his car knew the way to his house. All it required was his sitting behind the wheel!

I stopped drinking alcohol many years ago but my two friends continued with the habit. A few weeks ago, they were involved in a fatal accident that claimed their lives.

I was shocked on receiving the news though I had lived in fear that something bad would happen ever since the day the 'drunken driving lessons' started.

"What I did not expect to happen was something as dreadful as this, an accident that has claimed both the instructor and the learner,"

I was tearfully concluding my speech during their joint requiem mass, in one of the churches in Kisumu.

"As we celebrate the lives of my two friends, I sincerely apologies to their families," I gestured with my hand to where the two widows sat with their children, "………for doing nothing in stopping those lessons."

On the following day I attended their burial in Homabay.

The 'Rado' Watch

After I dropped out of school, I lived and worked in Nairobi. Those were the days when Dandora Estate, where I had a bed-sitter, was still a respectable and a safe place to live in.

Fifteen years down the line, the estate was different and one had to be careful before venturing into some of its areas.

The crime rate had gone up and one was always alert of an attack by pick pockets and other petty criminals. This was a far cry from Kisumu where life was still easy and fair. For the last few years I had more or less dug my roots in Kisumu and rarely went to Nairobi.

Recently, the fashionable wrist watch for those who had the means was 'Rado'. It is a heavy, gold plated watch. Only a few local businessmen could afford such a watch though every other Asian in town adorned one.

I was not among the lucky few local men nor was I an Asian. This watch was a luxury way beyond my pocket. This inability of owning such a watch did not kill my envy towards those who could afford such a masterpiece.

With this background you may excuse my excitement when such a watch was offered for sale at an unbelievable price.

I was in a bus to Kisumu and I had already paid the fare. The price the vendor was asking for was almost equal to the money that was remaining in my pocket.

After a lengthy negotiation, I was given the watch at a very fair price.

I arrived in Kisumu safely and for the next few days received compliments over my new watch. I felt good and where possible, I placed my hand in a way that the watch could be seen by those I was dealing with.

I was to travel back to Nairobi a few weeks later and I found myself in a dilemma over my precious watch. While I displayed it in the streets of Kisumu, the situation in Nairobi would be different.

I could even lose my hand as the thieves went for the watch! For security reasons, I had either to keep it in my pocket or leave it in Kisumu.

Anyway, I carried the watch and for the next few days moved it from the wrist to my pocket or vice versa depending on the security situation of the place I was in.

I met one of my brothers who lived in Nairobi during this visit and he casually looked at this watch and made no comment. I expected more than this from him! With disappointment, I kept my peace.

With him, we went to several places and I would remove and return the watch to my wrist as usual. In a concerned voice, he enquired as to why I kept shifting the watch from the pocket to my wrist. I explained my dilemma.

"I wonder whether anybody would be interested in your watch," he commented.

"Why? This is a 'rado' bro," I said in dismay. "Thieves in this city do not waste their time. They can tell a fake from a far."

I argued in defense of my 'rado' until he took me to a shop where real 'rados' were on sale. With amazement, I noted the difference not only in the price but on its quality. I left the shop feeling cheated and foolish.

Rather than keep this watch on my wrist since I now knew how valueless it was, I pushed it deeper into my pocket! I was too ashamed to put it on.

On my return to Kisumu, I sold it to one of my friends (of course at a profit). In turn, the new owner of a 'rado' watch thought that he had cheated me out as he hurriedly gave me the cash before I could change my mind.

This episode wizened me up and I no longer buy things from hawkers. It also got me thinking over what is really valuable. How truly valuable is what we deem valuable? Is it possible that we could even lose our lives guarding what is actually valueless? Could our aspirations and ambitious be geared towards what is in truth valueless? There is even a possibility that we paying dearly for valueless excess baggage!

I will Marry Rhoda in this Shirt

"Some of my earliest memories go back to the time I was seven or six years old." I confessed to my friend Pat.

"What is it that that you remember?" Pat prodded. We were chatting one afternoon after lunch, while relaxing under a tree outside our house.

Though heavy with a child, my wife had gone out of her way and prepared chapattis and beef stew, a meal she knew our friend used to like.

He was in Kenya for the first time after moving to America on winning a green card.

I was quiet, with my mind far away. "What are your old memories about?" Pat asked again.

We were discussing our days in our rural home as young boys. We had been neighbours and in many occasions did things together. For instance, we went to the same school, bathed and drew water from the same river and to crown it all, got circumcised on the same morning and by the same river.

Our chat had drifted to the girls we interacted with in those days. "I cannot recall whether I had started school or not but the scene is still very clear in my mind." I paused once again.

"We were outside our house and I had just taken a birth. Sitting under the eaves of our house were some family members together with a young lady who lived with us as a house help,"

"I was buttoning my shirt which was a Christmas present from my sister who worked in Nairobi. This new shirt made me feel proud and bold that I even talked of my innermost feelings."

"A week before that, I had attended a wedding and I was highly impressed by the smartly dressed bridegroom. I had that night dreamt of weddings where I was the groom while the bride was Rhoda, our house help. That dream and my smart new shirt may have prompted a declaration that was to haunt me for many years thereafter.

"I will marry Rhoda in this," I had declared innocently. Those around laughed which made me very embarrassed as it did any other time they teased me about it.

"Stop laughing at my husband," Rhoda had reprimanded them.

That innocent statement created a special bond between us and from that day on, she addressed me as 'my husband.'

"When I look back at that scene, I now see why my declaration was comical. Before them was a boy wearing a shirt long enough to cover his nakedness proposing to a girl who was definitely double his age.

Those were the days when boys wore no shorts and many of us wore a short on joining class one.

Even then, wearing a short was uncomfortable and I would remove it as soon as I arrived home. I would then put on my usual long shirt."

"Two years later, Rhoda married one of our neighbours and I was devastated."

I was angry with the man who had snatched the girl I intended to marry. What angered me most was that Rhoda had just moved to the home of her new husband without performing a wedding ceremony.

This was unbelievable to a 'man' who had intended to wed her in ceremony that could have been the talk of the village.

Days after the great disappointment, the new couple had visited us but their efforts in appeasing me with a present of sweets failed. I had held my hands behind my back as if to make sure that none of my hands got tempted into receiving the sweets offered. As they left after their uncomfortable visit, an attempt of pushing a coin into my shirt pocket also failed.

"How could that horrible man pretend to be my friend after eloping with my wife to be?"

Inheritance

I had not seen my cousin for some years though her home is not far from ours across the valley. Wambui is her name, a widow of sixty years. Her husband passed away a few years ago after ailing for some time. Their children are all adults and self-reliant.

From our home, one can see the tall blue gum trees that mark her homestead. These trees have been a source of income for her family for years but were directly connected to the problems that faced her. Together with his brother, her husband inherited the property of their late parents. Among them was a building in the nearby shopping center and the land on which they lived. A respectable number of coffee bushes grew on this land too.

The property at the shopping center was easily divided into two parts just as the land on which their homes stood. This could have marked the end of the inheritance process but an old stone house that belonged to their late parents stood on the part of the land inherited by Wambui's family. This house had to be shared by the two sons.

This could have been easy as well had a misfortune not befallen Wambui a few months after the death of her mother-in-law. One of the income-generating-trees fell on her house. Nobody was hurt but the earthen structure was destroyed together with the contents inside. With the consent of her brother-in-law, she moved into the old house which was now empty.

Wambui and her husband saw no need of building another house, and carried out some repairs on the old one. This was reasonable for the house stood on their land. They assumed that they would simply compensate her brother-in-law for his share. There was no fear that they could fail to agree.

The death of her husband a few months later was the end of their happy life. This is normal where a family loses a loved one. As she mourned the loss of her husband she lamented the loss of the opportunity of sorting out the few issues, which still hang loose, especially the fate of the house they now lived in.

For some time tension had grown between the two brothers, spreading to the rest of the family members. Physical confrontations had occurred severally between the sons on either side of the families. The intervention of the village elders had done little other than gross over the seething problem that lay beneath.

What was going to happen to her family that their main contact with the feuding brother-in-law was gone? As a strong Christian, Wambui believed that God would provide a way amongst all the confusion that surrounded her.

Wambui's husband was buried and the reasonable period for mourning was over. Life was to continue as normally as possible. Through an emissary, she sought a meeting with her brother-in-law with a view to sorting out the few inheritance issues remaining. The elders in the clan were invited to the meeting that took place on an afternoon, a few meters from the graves of their late parents.

The main agenda for the meeting was the fate of the old house. Wambui expressed her willingness in compensating her brother-in-law for his share in the house. She had the money and what needed to be agreed upon was the figure. She could not believe her ears when her brother-in-law stated that he had no interest in her money and all he needed was the physical division of the house itself.

"How can this house be divided up?" One of the elders enquired.

"I would like my share in the materials that make up this house."

"Are you suggesting that the house should be demolished and you share out the debris?"
"Yes"

Some of the elders tried to persuade him to accept the compensation in cash but their efforts were all in vain. All that he wanted was his share of the building material and not the money. The meeting was adjourned and another one slotted in the month that followed. It was hoped that by that time, the elders would have convinced him into accepting the more reasonable method of compensation.

Though it sounded unreasonable, her brother-in-law was within his rights in demanding for a share of the materials that made up the house. He even considered himself very fair for he was not asking for compensation for the rent that accrued in the period that Wambui had used the house!

Wambui had no alternative but to accept the unreasonable demand from her brother-in-law. She was given a period of six months in which to make arrangements for her accommodation.

I visited her home a few months ago and was ushered into a relatively new small house, a few meters from the site of the demolished old house. A pile of stones lay near the fence together with other assorted building materials. This pile marked the depth of the differences between the two families and the value of her share to the old house.

With a toothless smile, Wambui concluded the moving story by saying that she had forgiven her in-law and even loved him. This was hard to believe. She even allowed them the use of the path that passed through her property to the river. She argued that the man himself never fetched water from the river. It is the innocent children who would suffer in covering a longer distances in search of water. What could she achieve in punishing the children who had no part in the unreasonable decision made by their father?

"Cousin, vengeance is not mine, and my God knows of our suffering. Ours is to love those who hate us."

The Man Who Arose

"I could have taken a cup of tea if the attendant offered some," I declared raising a surprise from my cousins. "If you liked the environment so much, why don't you apply for the job they have been advertising?" In a voice full of sarcasm, one of my cousins responded.

It is true that a vacancy existed as the said adverts on the notice board had indicated. It is also true that I had lost my job a few months ago and I desperately needed a new one. However, what they advertised was not in my line.

"Thank you for the recommendation but that is not my career. Let me remind you that I am an accountant and there seemed to be very little accounting needed in that room." I was referring to the cold room of mortuary from which we had gone to collect the body of one of my cousins a few days ago.

The job that was being advertised for was that of an Assistant Mortuary Attendant.

I have a lot of respect for the people who work in these facilities because they handle the most solemn activities in our lives. However the possibility of working as mortuary attendant was beyond my imagination.

"What I really meant is that the environment in the cold room had been clean, and no foul smell hung around like in the last mortuary I entered," I explained.

That mortuary was at the Nyanza Provincial Hospital where the body of a relative was kept. The committee organizing his burial had assigned me, together with another two people the task of making sure that the body was well preserved. Those were the days before the emergence of private funeral homes.

I had tried to decline this assignment but my protest had been ignored by the chairman. Our task was to visit the mortuary in the morning and before the end of each day until we took the body for burial.

All the visits to the mortuary were horrifying with bodies strewn on the floor. We literally did a 'hop skip and jump' to reach the drawers where the body was kept. One of the bodies was rotten and what was remaining was a pile of bones.

The smell was depressing and it was a wonder that the attendant spent the better part of his day in that room. What I saw was a scene in a horror film.

Thus in following the orders of the funeral committee I visited this room twice a day for the next six days.

I came to learn that where such visits were not done the family of the victim would leave the body properly stored away but as soon as they left, the body would be removed from the fridge and placed on the floor. It would be returned to the fridge on the day the family came to collect it. In many case such a body would be in a bad state and smelling.

The atmosphere in the private mortuary was different with all the bodies decently stored away in the fridges which lined-up one side of the room.

There was hardly any smell other than that of the drugs used in cleaning and preserving the bodies. It was clean and orderly, a facility worlds-apart from the one I visited in Kisumu.

In response to my comment on the general

atmosphere of the mortuary, the attendant told us a story of one of his experiences.

"I used to work at the City Mortuary before I came here some two years ago," he was referring to the mortuary run by the City Council of Nairobi.

"The facility was in a deplorable state and it could hardly handle the flow of the bodies. In one night, ten or more fatal accidents would occur and all the bodies would be dumped at the mortuary."

He went on to tell us of how the bodies would be piled on top of one another as the harassed attendants sorted them out.

"One night, I saw a movement in one of the piles as one of the 'bodies' tried to free itself from the dead. I pushed the bodies away and freed a man who had been mistaken as dead. He explained that the man must have been in a coma after the accident and since many other had died in the bus accident, he had been assumed to be dead.

"Where am I," the man who had risen from the dead asked in shock.

Like in a dream, he realized where he was and slowly slipped back into a coma. He was taken to Kenyatta Hospital where he was treated and released a few days later.

Angela

There was excitement in the family in the few days towards the opening of schools all because of Angela who was joining class one. She had done a cat walk as she tried out her new uniforms and her beaming face showed how great she felt.

Monday being the big day for her new school came and Angela was among the very first to be up and ready. Though she usually had a good appetite, the excitement was too much and she could take very little of the breakfast laid for her. Off she went in company of the other children.

Adjustment in the new school was easy for she had the security of her other brothers and sisters in the same school. Apart from this, most of her former classmates made the majority of her new class. Angela enjoyed her day.

In the afternoon the little girl was bubbling with stories of her experience on her first day in school. "Mum, imagine auntie is a teacher." Angela confessed of her surprise on seeing her aunt among the teachers during the morning assembly. She was referring to her aunt who lived next door who taught at the same school.

"She is our teacher." The little girl was overjoyed by the turn of events.

Everybody in the family was surprised that Angela was ignorant of what her aunt did for a living. This is information she is assumed to have gathered as she grew up.

The Shepherds

"Why did she send me that far to take them lunch?" My sister wanted to know.

"I think she was concerned over their well-being," I defend my mother.

"I don't think so. My mum was not that kind of a mother. She could not have risked my life for the sake of two boys who were older than me,"

"Why not? The poor boys spent the whole day grazing,"

"Grazing what?" She asked.

"What do you mean? I believe there were goats, sheep and even cows in the flock," I was not sure of how big the flock was, but these are some of the animals usually kept in our area.

"What?" It was a miserable goat by the name Ngondi. Above all, what I took them was plain *githeri*, at times cooked the night before. The boys could have carried their food in the morning as they left,"

"What?" It was my turn to be surprised. I was hearing this part of my family history for the first time. I wanted to hear more.

"Ngondi was the first animal that our family ever owned and it was the mother of the goats we came to own later," my sister went on to tell the history of my family and its livestock.

"Before Ngondi was bought, my two brothers would spend most of their weekends and school holidays herding animals that belonged to our neighbours," she continued.

"As a way of putting their time into a more

economical use, my parents bought them a she goat.

"This goat was fed in its pen during the week when the two boys were in school. Over the weekends, and on school holidays, they would proudly take it out and join the other boys into the grazing areas which were a distance from our home. They would spend the whole day out and return in the evening."

"In the mid-day, my mother would send me to wherever they were grazing to deliver their parked lunch. This was usually a bowl of *githeri*," *githeri* is a mixture of maize and beans.

"Even in those days, I felt indignant that I was being sent all that way to deliver food to two boys who could have carried the food in the morning or better still came back for it later in the day. What didn't cross my mind then was the fact that all the hassle was in caring for a single goat! Today, it sounds very ridiculous and makes no economic sense."

"What bothered me was the danger I was exposed to." In my mind, I could see my sister as a little girl of may be ten years walking through the forest hugging a basket under her small arms. Those were the days when most of the country side was still bushy and infested with wild animals.

"I had this great fear of encountering a wild animal in the narrow dark pathway and it was a miracle that each day, I arrived safely at my destination. What I feared most were the hyenas which roamed the bushes and we used to hear their cry every night."

After miraculously delivering the food, my sister would dare not risk her life again by taking the journey back. She would stay till the end of the day. With time, Ngondi bore two kids and within a period of five years or so, the number of goats had multiplied into a sizeable flock. The herding business was no longer a hobby but an enterprise that brought milk and occasionally a goat for slaughter over Christmas.

Who Made the Decision?

"Who made the decision for us to settle in Kisumu?" My eight years daughter asked. She was not pleased with the person who made such foolish decision.

Though we were in the car with my wife, our second daughter and some three other relatives, I knew that the question was directed to us, her parents. I could not get an immediate answer and hoped that my wife would respond. After all, I was driving and my mind was occupied with the events of the last few days.

"Ask Papa," my wife responded shifting the burden of giving the answer sorely on my shoulders. I was uncomfortable and felt that my wife was being unfair.

I struggled with the answer as I tried to justify the reason as to why we had set our home in Kisumu. Deep in my heart, I knew that I would give a lousy answer and that my daughter would not be convinced.

Who really made the decision? I was still pondering. Ordinarily, we are wired in a way that we are relieved when we can shift the burden of blame to another person when things go wrong. As such we blame our parents on most of the things that are happening in our lives today. "My parents were poor and could not take me to a good school," "my parents divorced and we were raised by my mother," "my parents passed away and I grew up as an orphan." These and other countless circumstances can be attributed to other people and events.

As to the person 'who made the decision' for us to settle in Kisumu, I could point no finger at any one, least of all my parents. But just a minute, if my parents could have met the bill for my education abroad, maybe I couldn't have ended up in Kisumu or better still, if they used their influence and even paid the bribe that was being demanded for my admission to a local university, maybe I could have ended up somewhere else. In fact if that happened, I could have been saved from the agony of answering this question!

None of these 'may be' occurred and we were all rightfully squeezed in the car escaping from Kisumu. My daughters' question was fair and timely. For which self-respecting parent would make his or her family live in a city where thugs looted the homes and business premises of people from a certain community? To crown all, they set ablaze what they could not carry away. Such a parent had 'porridge' for brains or needed an examination in his or her head! I agreed with my daughter that such a parent was a fool.

We were escaping from the tribal clashes that followed the announcement of the disputed presidential election results of 2007 in Kenya. Hell broke loose and the rule of law was suspended for a time. Certain communities were targeted and their homes and businesses were looted and torched in different parts of the country. We, like many other residents of Kisumu and other towns, had stayed holed in our house for two days.

In those days, the volume of the T.V. had to be put down while the children could not play or even cry with the freedom they were used to. The lights had to be put off in the evening and the T.V. provided all the light we required. We sat and followed the news from both local and international stations. All the cameras were focused on Kenya as its citizens destroyed what they had built for almost half a century.

Everybody was scared. The children played their games with one eye on the T.V. and the other on the grown-ups around. Any sudden movement by one person translated into a scamper for everybody. Gun shots rang from all directions to our house and they sounded nearer and nearer. It was as if the combatants were pushing towards our home.

We lived in a double storey house and through the widow to one of the toilets, could observe one of the roads that led to the center of the city. Loads and loads of goods were being taken to a nearby estate by bicycle taxis. Those with no means of transport carried their loot in shopping bags.

In short, everybody was in a hurry taking their loot home. The real 'protesters' carried their wares in one hand and a machete on the other! They whipped the machetes on the tarmac producing a very chilling sound to their purported enemies. Among them were my two little daughters.

"Why are they sharpening the machetes?" the eldest girl had asked. Even for a child of her age, she could perceive the danger we were all in.

For how long were the tender minds going to be exposed to the on-going violence. Other than that, how long would I personally bear this torture? That night we prayed and went to bed though I slept very little. I also received an encouraging SMS from my Pastor Martin Mbandu asking us to read Psalms 91.

It gave me strength for it talks of an assurance

on our safety no matter the circumstances we are in. I knew that we would escape.

Our car had a little fuel and many of the petrol stations were closed while others had been looted. However, I hoped that I could get some if I woke up very early in the morning. By 3.00 am, I was in the city center which was quiet and desolate. It was not the Kisumu I knew. It was a ghost town I had seen in one of the movies.

Many buildings had been burned down, while others had been looted and their doors left hanging open. The streets were littered, and pieces of paper were blown away by the breeze from time to time. Of course there was no fuel in all the stations a passed through. I returned home deflated and hopeless asking God when the violence would come to an end.

"Would you like to drive with us?" This is the message I found in the house from one of our neighbours telling me that they were in their car ready to quit the city. I explained of my fruitless search for fuel but he assured me that he could drive behind as I sought fuel on the road to Nairobi.

Would I take the risk? There was no time to debate on it and within the next ten minutes or so everyone was awake and ready to go. We threw into a bag what we thought was necessary and departed.

As early as it was, the hooligans were awake and many parts of the highway were blocked with fiery burning tires. This put on hold any heroic actions like driving over the 'roadblocks'. At each of these 'roadblock', a wave of a few hundred shilling notes was magical and created a passage for us. A few kilometers out of Kisumu we managed to fuel and continue with our journey.

Of all the 'roadblocks' we had passed through, Sondu Township was the place where our lives were in real danger. It was around six in the morning and quite a big crowd was hanging at the 'roadblock'. I should explain that Sondu is built in a depression and that on its' approach from Kisumu, one has a birds' view of the shopping center. Even before we arrived at the 'roadblock' we met two men who were definitely running away from the violence. They warned us of the danger we were driving into. We were in a dilemma. In front of us was a mob that was not singing Christmas carols, while the one we had left behind were members to the dreaded Baghdad Boys! We drove on.

One of the mob members stopped us way before the 'roadblock' and greeted us in a certain preferred local language. To his surprise, we answered in Kiswahili. I guess he could tell from which community we came. With excitement, he shouted to the hundred plus mob, to come and join him in examining his rare find.

Before the mob could cover the short distance between us, a wave of a thousand shilling note, instantly turned him from an enemy into our protector. He safely herded us through the mob. That was the last 'roadblock' we encountered.

As we passed through, the words of the reading that Pastor Mbandu sent the previous night came into my mind (Psalms 91:9-130)

"...you have made the Lord your defender, the Most High your protection and so no disaster will strike you, no violence will come near your home. God will put his angels in charge of you to protect you wherever you go...."

I clearly saw the hand of His angel in finding fuel for our car and as we passed through the many road blocks. I also believed that an angel would be guarding the properties we had left behind.

As we drove towards Nakuru, we were all shocked when we realized that I had forgotten to carry most of the cash we had in the house. How could I have made such a silly mistake? Days later when I talked to my friends who had sought refuge in police stations I realized that that was not a mistake.

Some of them had cash in their pockets but their money could not buy food for their families or even fuel for their cars. It could not even pay for a decent accommodation. This is because all businesses were closed or looted.

God was telling us that our destiny was in His hands. He was telling us that money, which we often think is a solution to many of our problems, had no steering position in our life. God was in charge.

This became clearer and clearer till the end of the violence. While buildings and houses were being burned and looted, the three guest houses we operated were spared and continued serving the travelers trapped in Kisumu. They also acted as rescue centers for those with nowhere to run.

The house from which, we had hurriedly vacated, stood safe all through and we moved our belongings two months later. The cash we had left behind was still safe.

"It is God who settled us in Kisumu." I should have answered my daughter.

The Push

My family is young and we have been blessed with two daughters aged three and six. Though sibling rivalry rears its ugly head from time to time over toys and things, the two are protective of one another from any external threat.

We pass some of our evenings singing and telling stories where each of us is expected to do a presentation. Sometimes, rivalry arises between the two over the ownership of the songs they present. One of them could sing a song, which the other girl expected to present. The 'aggrieved' party would raise complaints that 'so, and so' was 'stealing' songs, spoiling the fun we could be having.

This 'theft of stories and songs' is inevitable even to the grown-ups. We may not quarrel and fight as my two girls, but some of us handle these 'stolen stories' in a deplorable manner. We retell and recount incidences as if we experienced them personally. These could be stories we have heard elsewhere.

I would not like to be accused of 'stealing stories'. As such, I retell a story I heard from a preacher in our church sometime last year.

An ancient king was looking for a suitable suitor for his daughter who was the heir to his throne. Those were the times when battles broke between his kingdom and its neighbours. In order to sustain his kingdom, more so after his own death, the 'queen to be', needed a husband who could lead in these battles.

After many days of considering the best way

in which to test the suitors, the King decided that swimming across a river invested with crocodiles was ideal. Driven by thirst and hunger for power, young men volunteered for the test whenever the contest was advertised. Many people, together with the King, came to watch the spectacle.

The young men jumped into the water but none of them survived the jaws of the hungry reptiles. Those who survived were maimed and disfigured that they could not fulfill the duties of a King.

Many days thereafter, another contest was organized and the eager crowd lined the riverbank. Nobody volunteered for the event and there was disappointment on the faces of the hither-to excited crowd.

As the last call was made for the braves to come out, the crowd pushed and jostled dangerously on the brims of the riverbank. Among this surging crowd was a young man who could qualify to be the suitor to the young queen if only he was brave enough to take the challenge.

However this young man had no desire of being the next meal for the ravenous reptiles. He was poor and preferred remaining so instead of losing his life altogether. Thus he stood on the riverbank among the crowd.

The anxiety among the crowd grew as each person craned his or her neck to catch the sight of the expected volunteer. The surge from behind pushed the young man off the bank of the river and in a splash, fell into the water. He was a good swimmer and though in shock managed to keep afloat. He surfaced a few meters away from the bank on which he had been standing before.

Between him and the bank he had been standing, a crocodile was swimming swiftly towards its next meal! The young man saw it and swam away from the menacing reptile. Devoid of any motive other than saving his life, the young man swam towards the opposite bank and mysteriously managed to dodge and out-swim all the crocodiles in that river. The crowd was in frenzy as they cheered the champion swimmer.

Though out of breath, the young man climbed to the safety of the opposite bank. While still wet, he took the nearby bridge and hurriedly returned to the bank he had swam from. There was continuous applause as he approached the crowd. Instead of heading to the dais, where the King was waiting to receive him, the young man went straight to the spot from which he had been pushed to the river.

"Who pushed me into the river?" The angry young man demanded.

His tone and the look on his face puzzled the onlookers. They did not belong to a person who was about to give a hug to the person who had pushed him into the river. To the contrary, they were murderous and chilling. No one could claim the responsibility even if a prize was offered. After all, the push had emanated from the rear.

As he raved with anger, the coordinator of the event came over and pulled him towards the dais where the royalty sat. The King congratulated him as the suitor to his daughter. The prospects of marrying the most beautiful and coveted girl in the kingdom sobered him up. He accepted the offer. Deep in his heart, he was grateful to the person who had literally pushed him to this good fortune.

Copy Cats

Ruth had been a teacher for many years in our rural area. Five years ago, a disaster befell her. Not that it happened all at once. It was gradual but its' effect was still devastating; she was losing her eye sight!

Within a period of four months, this lady who was a school teacher in a neighbouring primary school was almost blind. All she could see was a blur and just for a few meters. This was despite the frantic effort of saving her sight. She had visited all the leading eye surgeons but all had accomplished little. Their verdict was that she could lose her sight completely.

This was a desolate situation; person who had led her life independently was now a dependent. She had to get somebody to do for her even the simplest household tasks. This was the easy part, what would happen to her career as a teacher?

"My biggest worry was my career. I love teaching and was not ready to retire," Ruth was to reveal to a friend later.

"There were suggestions that I join the school for the blind, which did not appeal to me. I just believed that I would get well."

She received a lot of support from her fellow teachers who not only shared her work but encouraged her during those dark days. Though she was not getting better, the loss of her sight was on hold. With time, she got accustomed to her situation and the little she could see was enough to retain some normalcy in her life. She could see enough to take light duties in the junior school where the children knew of her situation and went out of their way in making her life easy.

It is now over eight years since she became partially blind and she has been able to adjust her life to this limited sight. Thus, she walks much slower than she used to, but she eventually gets to her destination. She also does all her household chores though slower and at times not as nicely as there before. What is important to her is the freedom she has regained.

In any level of learning, examination time is not the easiest for any student. It is a time of anxiety for many and the tendency of cheating is rampant. The students in Ruth's Junior School were not any special and the temptation of copying the work of a fellow desk-mate often appeared. This became tempting with the knowledge that their teacher could not see their actions.

"Can you imagine that when they copy their desk mates' work they copy everything, including the name of the pupil all the way to the answers?"

Ruth was to reveal to her fellow teachers as she tried to sought-out the papers. In front of her was a set of three papers bearing the same names! To make it more confusing, all the answers were the same. What a coincidence that three sets of papers had the same answers, though the hand writings were different. Apart from the three similar papers, two of her pupils had not submitted their papers though they had sat for the examination.

The poor copy cats could have escaped being discovered if only they were wise enough to insert their own names in their papers. After interrogation, they admitted that they had copied the answers and promised never to do it again.

The cleverness of these cheating students is like our own cleverness in the eyes of God. It is amazing that God through His Love is able to put up with our foolishness.

A Tribute to George

The Christmas season of 2007 was a busy one for Kenyans. Besides the hyper activities associated with this festive season, we were holding both the presidential and parliamentary elections. This is an exercise that we do every five years.

Kisumu City, like many other urban centers had lost a big share of its residents to the rural areas where many were voting from. In turn, this made the period a very unfortunate time to have a medical emergency.

A close family friend and his son had a road accident on the night of the twenty-fifth as they came from a late night Christmas dinner engagement. They collided with a matatu (Taxi) whose driver was too drunk to know that he was driving on the wrong side of the road.

They were rushed to one of the major hospitals in the city and received all the necessary emergency treatment. On the following morning, the son was discharged while his father, who was still in a critical condition remained behind. There was a general feeling that he was not receiving the best medical attention and the need of transferring him to Nairobi arose. In Nairobi, we all agreed, the patient would receive a specialized attention while near his family. The move was also hastened by the rising tension between certain communities in Kisumu.

I joined the family and friends who were keeping vigil at the hospital as the final touches on the plan to airlift George were completed. The flying doctors were to touch down at the Kisumu airport in the next few minutes and I drove with some three ladies to receive them. Also on the road to the airport was the ambulance which was to carry their equipment.

There was tension at the airport as the supporters of one presidential candidate insisted on inspecting the ambulance on its way out of the airport. Their fears were genuine for election-rigging materials could have been easily transported by air from Nairobi.

Back at the hospital, the crowd keeping vigil was growing and could have drawn attention had everybody escorted the patient to the airport. It was decided that only those who were directly involved in the transport of the patient would join the convoy. The drive to the airport was smooth and the flying doctors took off before the other regular flights.

As I talked with a friend who had just arrived, I saw the ladies I was with head to the car park. I followed them shortly thereafter but they were nowhere near my car. On looking around, I saw them comfortably settled in another car. This irritated me. Why were they so inconsiderate? I asked myself. Couldn't they have told me that they had found an alternative means of transport? I lamented. I drove towards the car they were in with an intention of bidding them a goodbye and at the same time, give them a piece of my mind.

When they saw me, they hurriedly left the car they were in and joined me. Their reaction surprised me and I took a moment in realizing that they had entered into the car purporting that it was the one we had driven in. They later explained that they found the car open, and parked at the exact spot in which I had parked in the previous visit. Moreover, its colour was similar to the car I drove, though the make different. We hurriedly took off before an alarm could be raised with regards to the mistaken car.

What could have happened had the owner found them in the car? Could he or she have raised an alarm? Or could its' owner have assumed that there was confusion on his or her part? Apart from this, how was its owner going to explain the chilled bottle of water, which my companions had left lying on the front seat. What about the empty one on the back seat?

We laughed all the way to town and anybody seeing us could have thought that we were coming from a party! Nobody could have associated us with the sad gloomy faces that had driven to the airport a while ago. Tears had been shed as the patient was hoisted into the aircraft.

I am glad that we tried all we could to save our patient. In a spirit of togetherness, money was hurriedly raised to clear the bill at the Kisumu hospital and for the charter of the plane. However, God had a greater plan for him. He called him to rest a few days later.

Baby Gacheri

In the land I grew, and I believe in many other rural areas in Africa, bread was a luxury that only a few could afford. In fact bread was a thing eaten by many on Christmas day and a must in a basket of a person visiting the village after a long sojourn in the city. On its arrival, we would eat it there and there.

Those were the days of the unsliced bread and each of us would be give a piece, plucked directly from the main body. We would eat it dry and in case it became too dry to swallow, chase it down with water.

I had heard that some people ate bread for breakfast but couldn't imagine how that was possible. If that was to happen in our home, we could spend a sleepless night waiting for the morning while imagining all the terrible things that could happen to our bread. For us, breakfast was tea or porridge and whatever remained from dinner the previous night.

Our fears were justified for one day my father had arrived home late in the night with a loaf of bread. We were asleep, and the bread was kept in the cupboard.

Those were also days when a cupboard was the place where valuable utensils, foods and drinks we were forbidden from eating or drinking were kept. It was usually locked with a padlock and all we could do was to salivate as we gazed at the delicacies through its wire meshed widow.

That night, rats which ruled our house the moment we went to bed, gained access to the cupboard, dug a tunnel into the bread and spent the rest of night feasting. In the morning, we found the bread wrapper and a few cramps of bread. We also found their droppings which announced their overnight feasting.

In those days, it was also common for my mother to reward us with bread in case we behaved well, or if one performed well in school. The same would happen during the coffee picking season, or if my mum wanted a particular task done. We could do anything at the promise of a piece of bread.

This brings me to my sister Gacheri, a toddler and her love for bread. She was around three years and I think I was around six and was yet to join a primary school. My mum would be going to the market, to river or even to the farm and Gacheri would wail as I restrained her from following her. After she was gone, Gacheri would insolubly continue wimping and I would do my best in re-assuring her that mum would come back very soon.

"Gacheri my baby, stop crying. Mum has gone to the market and she will bring you a loaf of bread," I would sooth my baby sister.

After a lot of persuasion, Gacheri would stop crying and most likely fall asleep. I would very softly roll her onto gunny bag spread under the granary. She was a heavy sleeper and she would at times sleep until my mum came back.

You may be wondering why we slept under the granary while there were beds in our house. This was because we were too young to be trusted with the access to the house. As such, the house would be locked and our food and drinking water left in the granary. As for our napping, we would crawl to the space below it.

The time of my going to school came and there was no one to take care of Gacheri when my mum went away. However there were places where mum could not go with her and whether 'she shed blood for tears', as my mum used to say, Gacheri would at times be left alone in the compound albeit for short durations. In all these incidents, she would cry herself to sleep.

In one incidence, I spied on her soon after my mum left and what I heard her mumbling in her toddler voice drove me to tears.

"*Gacheri witu, tigakurira, mami niegukurehera mugate,*" my dear Gacheri stop crying, mum will bring you a loaf of bread. Gacheri was soothing herself to sleep. Those were some of the words I used to sooth her with. After a few moments I saw her craw under the granary and fall asleep.

Like Gacheri, each of us need that in-built ability of encouraging and consoling ourselves because at times our family, friends and even the community we live in will fail us.

'Pupu'

Vicky was three years old and her elder sister Nelly was five. We lived in Kisumu's Mountain View Estate and with my wife, we ran a guesthouse. We were comfortable in our way and thanked the Lord for what was happening in our lives.

Vicky was yet to go to school and spent most of her time home with Janet, our house help. Janet was a responsible girl and we had been together for the last two years. That was a long period in comparison to the other house helps who had stayed with us. Some hardly settled down before demanding their pay and leave.

She had progressed well in her 'potty' training and our budget on diapers had gone down. At most, she could hold her horses until she reached her potty.

After she did her business, the messy part of disposing the 'pupu' begun. She would inspect her performance and if she did well, expected to be congratulated!

There were occasions when she cried with frustration for not producing any 'pupu' at all!

She was excited when she produced a handsome load of 'pupu', and if I was home, her joy would not be complete until I saw the results of her efforts. Though the 'pupu' had a foul smell, I still inspected her work and even congratulated her.

In most cases, I took the potty and passed it over to the person who would do its disposal. She had no problem with this though she felt that she could have done the job better if given the opportunity!

For a reason better known to Janet, she one day ignored the usual protocol and turned my house into a 'small Mogadishu'. Vicky had done her part, her bottoms were wiped and her respectability restored.

She had picked her potty and was bringing it over to me for the usual inspection. I was in the sitting room with a visitor, and may be, this could have prompted Janet to wrestle the potty from Vicky's fragile hands.

Vicky wailed as she fought for the recovery of the potty. In the process, the mess was spilled on the floor.

I made my way to the war front and said the correct words in soothing Vicky and after a short time peace was restored. My visitor had heard the chaotic proceedings and I guessed that he was keen on knowing what the cause was.

As I filled him in, I saw the importance that the young girl put in the task of showing me her 'pupu'. On the other hand I saw the uselessness that Janet saw in the action. To Vicky, parading the 'pupu' was a matter of life and death.

In this incident, I saw God's Love to mankind in a more spectacular way. Though we may be as worthless and vile as the contents of the potty, God stills loves and cares for us. This confirms that man is special in the eyes of God. Why then do we feel inadequate? Why do we allow those around us to make us feel useless?

THE END

9 789966 133779